Fantasia for the Man in Blue

Fantasia for the Man in Blue

Tommye Blount

Four Way Books
Tribeca

More Praise for Tommye Blount

"I have been waiting for this miracle of a book to come out for so long
without understanding why—until I was finally allowed to read it
from start to finish, first in one big gulp, then slower, with the kind of
leisurely pleasure I might otherwise reserve for dessert. Pay attention to
the lyric lightness, the vivid and philosophical diction, the keen function
of form, the grasp of history and its consequences. Then indulge in the
satisfaction in language, the refashioning of myth, and, perhaps there is
no other way to say this: the STYLE, honey. Tommye Blount is one of
our greatest writers because he is willing to do what is so difficult: hold
poems to exacting and crucial standards. This book was written not by a
master, but a virtuoso."
—Tarfia Faizullah

Library of Congress Cataloging-in-Publication Data

Names: Blount, Tommye, author.
Title: Fantasia for the man in blue / Tommye Blount.
Description: First edition. | Tribeca : Four Way Books, [2020] |
Identifiers: LCCN 2019031755 | ISBN 9781945588495 (trade paperback)
Subjects: LCGFT: Poetry.
Classification: LCC PS3602.L679 F36 2020 | DDC 811/.6--dc23
LC record available at https://lccn.loc.gov/2019031755

This book is manufactured in the United States of America and printed on
acid-free paper.

Four Way Books is a not-for-profit literary press. We are grateful for the assistance
we receive from individual donors, public arts agencies, and private foundations.

This publication is made possible with public funds from the
National Endowment for the Arts

and from the New York State Council on the Arts, a state agency,

We are a proud member of the Community of Literary Magazines and Presses.

Contents

This is what makes me feel niggerish, I'm afraid: being watched.

Fantasia for the Man in Blue

You know good and well you can't be out here
in the dark morning to take in

the moon—full as the bowl of light
attached to this police cruiser. Like a grayed
elephant shoots air through its trunk

before it charges off to safety
from a mouse in one of those old black
and white cartoons, you shriek

in a debutante's pitch,
even though, there are reports,
you are as large as an elephant.

Car thefts in the area,
the man in blue explains after
he asks, "Where do you think you're going?"

It's unusual to see your kind walking
at this hour. You're an elephant
who's really just a man sweating away

in a mascot's costume. You mumble
an address; you fumble
for an address that isn't *your* address

but mine. Oh, you've done it now—
don't say anything else. Let me
take over this body; soften what letters

will bend—I am a poet after all.
Don't worry. You'll see. He'll wish us
a good morning and let us go,

after he bends us over the black hood.

I

How Sweet this Great Land

The white girl is arrested
by joy—or is it hunger?

Whatever is there bubbling
in her perfect little body,

she has been taught
to subdue it. Crossed,

her arms make an X
like a contract's signature; her wrists

rest against her skirt's pleats.
Almost as if I were a lecherous savage

and not the coheir of this
moment, my nose brushes

the photograph—*what must her hands
smell like?* Not an odd question

when I consider the dangers
of hunger. Ah yes, there it is—the scent

too loud for even history to shush:
sweet relish, sharp chives, crush of dill—

sandwiched under her nails; a sandwich
some Black child's mother made. How sweet

this great land of nostalgia—
when there were fewer

houses than there were trees;
safe. She looks as if she might hum;

so happy to be in the cool shade
of the man swinging from his branch.

Americana Elegy

Less boy, more band,
more twang, less bling,

less hip-hop, on brand,
more opry, less bang,
less cornrows, more corn-

field, spiritual, less house,
more plantation, a shorn

image, more downhome,
more green, more blue
sky, more bluegrass,

less rhythm, less
blues, more church pew,

more cross, less hood,
more hood, more white
washed denim, less back-

lash, more goldenrod,
less ballad, more lyric,

less gold grills, less rap
sheet, more sheet music,
less trap beat, less trap

beat, more poplar,
less popular, a more authentic timbre,

more big game, more field
dressing, more lake,
more master—control.

My God, Lick Him Clean

After "Portrait of Christopher D. Fisher, Fourth Reich Skinhead, 1995,"
   Peter Williams

"Who is *this*," you asked
yourself, then swiped right
across the white boy's face.
And the rest was history.

It's immense—larger than Williams' canvas;
larger than the skinned head of that framed white boy
staring back. I'm talking an old big boat,
a Portuguese schooner named Arrogante.

It's an old story: the ship trucked
its swiped cargo all the way from Sierra Leone
only to be captured in Montego Bay.
In the hull of the ship, a boy

whose skin and hair were brighter than any
the sailors had ever seen before. Out of curiosity or love
of ritual from the old country, they held him down;
pulled his head back

—the neck opened faster than his wrists or ankles.
If you were there, you would have mistaken his begging
for song, you would have heard the splash
of their laughter. You should have seen

the head, its brilliant blond halo, put out in the Atlantic.
Oh, you too would have found yourself in the hull of the ship;
hungry. Bad horse meat, you would have said.
You'd never be able to get the blond strand

out of your teeth. Refuse to eat and the men
would have made sure you never hungered
again. As a charm or votive to God, the men,
before eating it, held that boy's heart in their hands

the way Williams' white boy has yours now. Now, don't go worrying
your pretty little head, all of that stuff happened a long time ago.

　　　⁓

　　　　A long time ago, after the white boys in blue
　　　　beat Rodney King, I was there watching

when the Black boys dragged Reginald Denny
from his truck; my face was cast in the television set;

my face, an American intersection, the black sun
of my face burned into four Black sons;

An old story: once you fell for a blond boy
with black suns for eyes; fell to your knees,
put him in your mouth. It was immense,
you could not breathe. He held your head

down there for so long. Oh, he couldn't help it
that he was so beautiful. Why would he want you
to lift your head, meet his gaze in the middle of it—
a reminder of what you both were to each other.

That's an old story—one in which
your body became nourishment
for his. You didn't resist
when he held your head down,

your nose pressed against his pelvis,
his head buried in your throat
an old salve. He couldn't help it,
that boy was so sweet, so devastatingly pretty.

~

Whose face is this?

~

my eyes, the crowns of their heads; my face,
many faces in the crowd—it was an old story,

historical, there was no difference; we all looked alike,
no one could tell whose face was whose,

~

An eye for each soft eye—are they not guilty
of innocence? The face swiped
across the canvas could be anyone or no one—
simply a mask staring back. In the portrait

of the subject, always the likeness of its maker,
there is no difference between *you* and *me*.
It's your painted face, a blackened face,
that can't stop smiling, you're the skinned

head, the one the white boy held
between his legs until you lost your Black mind,
until you choked on all of that whiteness, blond hair
caught in your teeth. It's a story heard before,

but you wanted to save the white boy
from history, so you begged him to use your body;
let him call you his salve; make you his
absolution. When he tells you he's sorry,

how could you not fall to your knees,
my God, lick him clean?

            when we dragged that white boy to his knees,
            we dragged all white boys

who have trucked their way through history;
we dragged him as if we meant to save him

from his whiteness; we wanted
to skin the skin right off of him,

~

Who *is* this, you ask the face, because you can't see
the race. It could be anyone staring back—
the tendons woven back over then across
themselves like history's ashen fibers.

No, not across, just underneath the surface,
always there ordering each cord to raise
or fall, like when a Black man opens his mouth
wide enough to accommodate a white boy,

of course, the way you did, the history around your lips
tensed, then slackened like rope or a noose or
a tied knot. You wanted to marry your body with his
until there was no difference between *you* and *me*.

Who was it that said: in the portrait of the subject
is always the likeness of its maker?

~

Whose face is this, whose face is this?

~

so many witnessed the white man's skin,
soft as history, how it gave up, how it caved,

how it surrendered his skull, how we recognized the face
of every white man that took shortcuts before him;

when we were done, he was unrecognizable; we were infamous,
the L.A. Four, we made a name

~

Christopher: the name of Williams' white boy
is the name of the white boy who
pressed your head down on his little head,
then you bared your teeth a little, enough

17

to eat him, he wanted it to hurt a little—
a little forgiveness that was not forgiveness,
he wanted you to scar him a little,
give him something tangible enough

to heal from, it's an old story, you gave him what he wanted,
you did not heel your big Black mouth, you were always hungry,
he made sure you were never hungry again,
he flooded your mouth, and (see?) you did not drown,

your throat clear enough to sing: *O my white longing,*
O my long pig. You were not the past,
you were past racial, so you sucked his long pig
to divorce him of his kin, to force all of him in your mouth;

his blond head thrown back as if he might laugh;
his face swiped in shadow; his eyes shut to history's cuckold.

    ⁓

    for ourselves; we got that white boy on all fours,
    he couldn't talk, we made him swallow

his words; he wasn't innocent; we were wronged;
okay, we didn't *drag* him, but he *climbed out* of his truck;

why didn't he stay inside; why didn't we stay inside;
why did he have to face us; why did we have to face him;

who did he think we were; who did we think we were;
we made him sorry; we were sorry;

he called out for help; we were calling out for help;
we were just kids; I was just a kid—

my mouth wide open, I swallowed
the Black boys, I swallowed the white boy,

I held my head down, I choked up, I was so sorry—
whose face was that; whose face is this?

~

There is no difference between *you* and *me*.

~

I am in love with a white boy, he is beautiful,
so sweet. You should see him, I mean really see him:
the way his head gets framed inside the crook of my neck;
my nose pressed against his forehead.
When he holds his hand to my chest,
a salute against my heart,
is this not a pledged allegiance, a vow, love
of ritual from an old country?
Let's call this an epithalamium—
an old story about balls and chains,
one you've heard before. Through the blinds'
slats, the sun catches his face and
he is so beautiful. I lose my breath
when he pulls my head back,
my eyes meet his eyes and I want to drown
in them. My Black suns in his eyes.
I give him my heart.

I've lost my head, it's an old story.

Whose face is this; whose body falls now from my mouth?

~

History: Arrogante: big boat: swiped cargo: swipe right.

~

I can't speak. Whose tongue is in my mouth?

The Button

I didn't quite suit him, so my brother
—without a word, as if it were his shirt—
popped my top button. I grabbed him by the
wrists—the same way I do all men hurt

by a need to fix me, sieve out the honey from my blood.
I meant to break him like the sweet promise
I'd make to any lonely man—horny
enough to break to me the same promise.

Do we, in our hold, this hug, this pushing,
not appear as feuding lovers? Brothers,
yes, yes, are nothing but lovers passing
blood back and forth in one fight, another.

He could've loved me, so I let him prevail.
Instead, he flicked a piece of me from his nail.

The Purse Thieves

There was the arm, the black
pricey number barely on her

white shoulder in broad daylight.
Why first did she have to look

to *my* face when she screamed
stop? I did nothing

except look up from the gas pump,
yes—held tight as a gun,

before I looked back down again to witness
nothing, only my shadow. I saw nothing—

just two boys who favored me
when I was that age and always mistaken

for being older. I mean, I felt nothing,
except that my body was not my body

anymore; stomach shoved aside
to make room for two more; I was an animal

raised to be slaughtered in the name of a
pricey leather number dangling from a shoulder

to be stolen. It all happened so fast—
my shadow bled into their shadows,

for a moment, a second, an eye-blink,
as we fled across the lot. We

were at play together in a race
like brothers. And like brothers,

just like that, the shadows broke apart
and we were separated again. I saw nothing—

only their bodies
slid into the back of a white van and

I slid back into my white car
as if I might chase them down

to save them or
I don't know. I did nothing,

I brought both hands to my face.
I heard the white van's wheels peel the afternoon

like a mask I thought could never be removed—
a skin. When the police sirens grew larger,

I pulled my hands from my face,
placed them on the steering wheel.

Historical Site

Still it's dark enough
this morning that I can see
the fireflies going off and on—
recording what angles
the old house's cameras cannot
see. *Something* is watching me,
so I keep my distance
when I strain my eyes to read
the lit plaque
to the left of the front door.
My eyes are useless;
vision not good enough
to parse out what part of history
is important enough to warrant
bronze foundry. I overheard at Meijer
one day that some part of this house
was used to hide slaves until nightfall
when they'd follow the stars
south of here, to Canada. As often with history,
this house has been restaged. Not even the land it squats on
is the original address, the house lifted
from its foundation
a mile down the road,
yet it makes for a lovely setting for white

weddings, picnics, guided tours.
I'm afraid of this big house
when it is dark like this;
when *I* am dark like this.
Not a slave, I can read
and want to run
my finger across the raised lettering,
even though that would trigger some alarm;
would flood the yard with white light;
would signal the police to come
and the police would flood me with white light—
so many stars spangling all over me.
I'd be the constellation those runaways
angled their necks up to—
blinking and blinking.

Late Show at the Americana

I

Oh, you know America—there was a decision:
sell off the small house to the big house;
add metal detectors; shake every purse;

reverse every pocket—what's that in your pants;
take off your coat, your shoes; nope, you can't
wear those—get them socks off; better yet, take off

your shirt—that one too; step out of your pants; drop
the underwear; keep your eyes on me—
I need you to pay attention; part your hair

then your cheeks, your ass; lift your balls,
lift your tongue; tell me where you parked
—I need to search your car for something;

I need to drive your car to your house;
give me the keys to your house or I will have no choice
but to knock your door down; where is the thing—

under the sink; under the floorboards; you don't
need to know what I'm looking for;
I've got my reasons; you can come in

over my dead body; once you exit
who's to say I will let you back in?

II

If you wanted to return, a ticket
is not enough, my friend—it's just

a slip of paper that can be torn.
Look here, give me it—

see? Now try to get past me—
I dare you. I'm a fucking wall, dude.

Respect the badge—this star
with my name written across it.

III

Flicks are my thing—ask me anything. Like,
I bet you didn't know this: the horror house

in this movie, that's set in Birmingham, Michigan,
was actually a plantation-style house in Birmingham,

Alabama. Isn't that wild; the way one part of America
can stand in for another part of America?

That's like if I called you nigger
in Birmingham it sounds the same as if I called you

nigger in Birmingham. Of course, I would never
say that word, you understand. I like you people.

IV

Just bury me in this blazer,
these starched pants, licorice dark shoes.
Or better yet burn me up, then

pour my ashes in a film reel's canister.
Bury *that* in a block of cement; pour me

into the sidewalk the way they do in Hollywood
with the stars on the Walk of Fame. It's American,
the dream to leave a piece of you behind

for tourists to walk all over. Look down
at the ground—you are standing in

my home. You know what I say? Shut the door behind you
when you leave *my* country of screens;
of so many white stars.

V

So these fucking dudes, that don't even speak
English, keep carrying away my theater brick by brick,
right past me as if I am so white
that I've disappeared—no one sees me.
I refuse to move; I can't leave—
my counter always ready at zero, zero, zero.
Have you heard of those multiplexes now?
They want you to believe those
tiny shit boxes are just like home: La-Z-Boys
that recline to a fuck-me friendly angle; shitty food like
fried mozzarella sticks and potato skins; more showtimes:
all to get more bottoms for their bottom lines.
Oh, I know America. Oh say can you see
my wide white ass—it ain't going
anywhere. This is the house of dreams I built.

VI

Where the balcony was, a sign went up
for a Starbucks; the ticket booth, a Korean-owned

nail shop. You should have seen
how they carried away the screen—

a bridal train without a bride. And me here,
a groom jilted at the altar, all dressed up

funeral-nice. Remember when a movie
was one big screen: one image shared by many:

black and white? The movie house
was a country of star gazers—all in the dark

looking up into all of that light.
And everyone knowing their places.

Framing Debra Shaw

I felt as if my body was in a picture frame.

A simple math of angles really,
nothing too fussy, a square,

soldered at each corner a ring, sound
design, just thin enough not to be confused

for shackles, there are no chains,
little bangles to meet her biceps,

garter her strong upper thighs, see
there is room for her to slip out of them

if she chooses, McQueen asked,
she had a choice, okay,

okay?, okay?!,
she was made aware of the frame, open

to opening the show, to show,
McQueen said, Aryan notions

of beauty are ridiculous,
so why not open—her body

as the entry way, her walk
barely a walk, an animal-scuttle,

does she even feel it, when her thighs
pedal her down the steps, is there an ache,

her soles slosh the runway—filled with black
water, it isn't that deep,

a tributary to hop across, or
a mouth opened to trouble

the hound-eyed cameras'
sniff for the smell of

genius, everyone claps
for her, or not for

her, the simple black
mesh dress, its beaded fringe—

how, as graceless as she appears,
she manages

not a rip or tear, isn't it a miracle,
McQueen's folly, his imagination,

a savagely dark and beautiful thing?

Proscenium

If skin is a stage's scrim through which
light passes and drums up
what the eye wants to see, then
the body is a theater

of war—a site of
disagreement between what is
there and what one
perceives is there. There is a town

on TV coming undone
over the body of a boy
believed to be devoid of light. The town
disappears in light after explosion

of light projected through
the television set to my eyes—
refusing to look closer.
If I were to look closer

at the scene, there would only be
a series of red, blue, and green
pixels abutting each other
like the political map

of this city or that village. Inside of the TV,
the protesters are struck by the song
of nightsticks and pepper spray, then they turn
into smoke screens. In that case, then, the body

is a smoke screen for what
I lack the courage to say:
if that boy devoid of light ran toward me
would I have not flinched, in return,

with my body—devoid of light?

The Laugh

Could he have had a prettier brown mouth?
His teeth made the warmest smile
when he fetched one fish

from its pocket of ice,
crushed. I could have
a crush on a man

with a smile like that.
A man's mouth, when caught
in between words,

can be so delightful
when he laughs,
leaves just enough room

for his tongue to worm through
straight-straight teeth,
before they snap down again

to bite back a moment
of giddiness. I should've kept
my Black faggoty mouth shut.

A man with a laugh
that deep must be starved
for a good punchline like this one

I have become. And who am I
to deny him of joy.
I could learn to kiss a man with a mouth like that.

Phonophobia

Body cam footage, the crackle and chirp of it anyway, I'm within
earshot—I know what is about to happen

again; click the news site's window closed; open my window
to geese barking a path across the man-made pond,

the pond plopped near a quiet suburban lane. One flops over, pops up
with a spray of grass in its beak. It turns its bearded head away

to the road's new pitch—an ice cream truck blares the white noise
of an old American song. The tune whips the air

in my mouth into vanilla soft serve. Once, back in Detroit,
my brother sent me out to shout for the Mister Softee truck.

Two cones. "So I said: *Little Brother, where is the other cone?*
You should have two," he always starts and upon hearing the beat,

I chime in with, "So then I said: *I had two but yours went splat*
on the ground. I just started slurping away on the other cone."

None of this ever truly rings a bell for me, I never remember
yet want to remember, so I rattle off the learned script,

so that he can laugh, then I can laugh harder,
which makes him laugh even harder until we both

bark and crack up with tears streaming down our faces,
we are so happy then: the guffaws, the chuckles,

just one big snicker, we can't stop laughing, we laugh until we can't
breathe, you'd think we are dying.

At the Mercury Theater,

in closeness that can only be had
through what harms, a man

steps on the toe of another man's
Nike by accident. In this city of driven men,

a man can't have a thing without another man
settling his weight on him first. On the ceiling

above it all, traced into deities,
stars. *They're shooting, oh my god,*

someone bored with the movie's squibs shouts
when there is no gun,

and the men take it out
into the lobby, then out

onto the sidewalk
under the marquee's Hollywood grin,

each of its teeth a letter,
misnomer of the true bloodbath

the audience is after.
They circle the men. Cry.

Whoop the way fanatics
do for autographs. Matinee idols

baring their chests, it's too late
to call them anything

except lovers kissing
their fists in a show of love

of what comes after love.

Blood Harmony

After a scene from the Rainer Fassbinder film Querelle—
an adaptation of the Jean Genet novel Querelle of Brest.

This will be anything but beautiful—
blade-buried in us, bloodshed,

or rather the need for it in all the ways
we, I'm told, should crave love too.

To loathe, heir of my father's blood,
is the matter of sentience: I know

I am meant to love you, yet can the salt
of our blood's serum be the elixir to break

this fever of rage; this kissing
of fists? Are we not at war over my body,

its dominion—which men may stroke my arm
and which cannot?

Here is my mouth, give me the sweet
ache of your knuckles. Let's unravel

our mouths in the most dangerous song
of fraternity; fill our ears

with nothing except each other; with scales
for which our bodies, together,

are the only capable instrument;
a fine instrument of brutality—

a double-minded man of muscled
rage, reluctant tenderness. We dance

around that which we are only brave enough to signal
with our blades' short and bright lyric. Skilled

as we are in the blood-bother of this evasion,
we mean only to stifle the air

of one another—momentarily; to be sensed
as if we matter to the other; to be reviled

only to be revealed, at last, relieved
of this anger's load. Now we have locked hands. Joined

is your right to my left—do we mean to harm
with this one fist? It kisses

no mouth. It promises only to break
open our desire to be touched and consoled

in a way only a brother's hand can.
Brought here by the blood deed

of brothers, I can't turn away
in cowardice or shame from your need

to prove the point of your blade's sentiment
for a body's revision. You and your consort,

this sharp-tongued brother, mean to break
me; lathe me down with its lipless kiss

into the brother you wished you inherited.
By the blade's argument, I am to be nobody

or a new body—a new brother pulled from harm's
kiln. Isn't that the glory of wounds and the breakage

of bones? Their eagerness, I mean, to heal.
What has harmed before becomes a science

of fear: the body postured awkwardly
in its attempt to avoid the same old errors,

old behaviors. Go on then, school me
on what blood is for, yet know my blade too

has its claims on your body's hagiography.
Now, it wants to question a tree

down your face; to mark your beauty.
At the center of love is always buried a blade's head.

The Pool

I dared look at nothing except the horizon line
where the russet tone of my brother's ankle

met the pale tone of his well-paced heel,
his flip-flops smacked the wet tiles,

though they barely rippled the puddles
that flowed toward the unseen pool

and its vinegary blue—
I smelled it, it burned my chest

the second I let my gaze break
from my brother to the lather

broken in a naked man's hands,
it could have been a toy,

that small, I mean, a little blue boat
capsized in his hand,

god-like, as if it was nothing,
and I was nothing

to hide from, I wished
he would get on with it,

destroy this little vessel,
a storm to wash me,

a disturbance

in the way a still body of water,
so easily, gives up its stillness

for what slips from the hands
of a bad yet careful boy

by accident—or
is it on purpose: a thing meant

to be hidden or lost,
so as not to be bothered with,

but my brother,
unlike me, didn't want

to lose me, my eyes trained back
down on his heel,

his grip a little tighter,
my fingers already burning, blue.

II

Fantasia for the Man in Blue

It's the great blue hero,
elephant-trunk

hung, chewing the set
and every man in it

like the big star—
a convincing replica

in the distance video
promises—

he flashes before he
flashes his long

nightstick at hustlers
and car thieves who know

I want as much as you do now,
touching yourself; pretending

the man in blue would bend over
backwards to protect you from

the boredom of your unremarkable
penis. You get off on this

even when it isn't on screen
in front of you, all in your head.

Let's say you're a criminal;
you fit the description;

you did everything
of which you are accused.

Now, say there is a deal
on the table, then, imagine that,

you are on the table.
And like evidence,

a bargain, if you let him,
he swallows you,

promises to forget the whole
thing. Say you let him cuff you.

Every address ending in "sir,"
the way your father taught you.

Leroy Auditions for the Fame School

Oh, they never should have told me
to cup my hands over my eyes.

The kind of boy I was,
I knew all too well

our bodies are tricky
constructions. So little, I knew

my body's argument
for wanting to want

could not be trusted,
but where did he come from,

Leroy, barely in a shirt, hardly in gym shorts,
wielding a sneer that makes even Debbie Allen

swoon *wicked*. Wickedness
is something, today, I have mastered—

no? Ask me now and I will tell you
the names of every muscle it took

for Leroy's waist to roll him
from one end of that parquet

to the other. What did I know
about him then, that they didn't

think I knew already? Bodies
are not walls—

shield us from what?
Oh, bless their hearts,

I watched all of his pieces
trouble themselves apart

only to resolve themselves
back together through

hands not large enough
to shield a thing like desire.

Did they not see my feet
pedaling the air

as Linda Clifford sang,
"I work so hard to get me a man.

Don't try and take him away."

The Ballad of Bobby Blake

I'd think it hard to sort the harness;
how it comes undone: a maze
of leather, each weathered strap passes
under then through, but always

ending up where it started. The O-
rings' eyes have failed to see you
for whom you mean to be now—no,
not the obsidian statue

so many white men have desecrated
themselves before, mouths filled with *god*
and *god, plow me* under what light your bald head
does not eclipse. You are not their bleak

god, no more center of the reversed-bukkake,
enough of your body's wine to feed
all of them—those blue-eyed hound dogs
begging for mercy, because they've misled

their master's search for you.
You're not *their* man
anymore, you want the blue
bowl of a baptismal pool, a hand

to pull you under. Father, O,
father of hunger, show me how you
escaped the harness' last buckle, its *No*.
Did the frame fall like an old god's statue

or a new groom's mouth, for the first
time, saying a new surname? Or was it like a fang
releasing its own hide, when the prong
let go, at last, its worn hole?

Castro Supreme Finally Speaks

Man, as long as the deposit clears,
I'll be a white boy's

dare; his rough scat;
the hood

he thinks he's discovered.
Let him tell the other white boys

I'm nothing but meat;
let them meet me on camera;

let them say it to my face.
I'm a beast, nigga; a cash cow;

a big show; a big tell.
I touch their hair

to yank their heads back
so they can see me.

I tell them how good they feel.
Tighter than pussy the white boy

behind the camera has me say.
Yeah, I let *him* tell me what to do;

he directs my yellow ass toward the shine
of all those coins. The white boys can't touch

my dick unless they eat it.
I make them eat it;

tell them how good it feels
to hear them cry

like little bitches.
My shades stay on—

they can't look me in my eyes.
Naw, they can't kiss me,

I'm a real nigga.
They can't fuck me.

They want it bad. I don't need
a lot of words. I know

my place, move when I'm told.

Ode to Chub Porn

To enlarge the frame, sure,
you could open the window wider,
though what is the point,
the men will just spill over,
their bodies are too big
to take in all at once,
the girth of them would never
fit, they are well-lit
like the stingy physiques
of Grecian statues, no,
just take in every aching line,
crave what's around the bend of each curve,
where you didn't realize
a man could have body,
body, a world gone mad
with here-and-here,
and here, no matter how much
you take in, there is still more
man to be addressed,
you need a generous accommodation
for these husbands of more-more-more,
so much more they could teach you
about the measure of your mouth,
its little impossible hole,

how it can starve a man to death
if it isn't big enough,
there is no such thing as *enough*,
they are so big, it's a shame
your bandwidth is too small.

Not an Elegy for Erik Rhodes

You could have just as easily fit another body
inside this poem that isn't

a white man—shaved
and muscular—

whose storyline, it seems, is always
to be the cop with a weakness

for the perpetrator pinned
to the ground in such a way

that it sounds as if he
cannot breathe, the throat locked

under the glazed forearm.
The perpetrator is Black

and so are you, yet you insist
on giving the shiny star another scene

in which to shoot
his wad one more time,

when the scene of the crime
is full of wadded bodies,

whom you too could be mistaken for, shot
then shot on video in another kind

of blue movie. Tommye, don't you wonder
if you've worshipped his white body enough

by spilling yours?

Diesel Washington Demonstrates *The Bully*

The white boy is not a fucking victim,
he's in on it too, he's done this before,
we have a history, he wanted me

to teach him how to do it for the film,
we rehearsed with clothes on, before the erection
of the set, before the fluffer could whet us,

the key light cold, no one to witness,
witness in that way one witnesses a
schoolyard brawl: a circle of boys

watch two boys have at it
as if there is no one watching them
open each other up in ways only

a boy knows how to do to boys.
I make it look dangerous, lift him up
in a headlock, his feet rise off the floor,

but he's the one in control,
all his weight on me. When he feigns his yells,
the men in blue can't come quick enough.

Thug on Thug

You see the way the bottom looks
back over his shoulder to his top
in what Pornhub promises to be a scene
that looks nothing like brotherly

love? I love the way this makes me
rewrite some mythic story
in which the poet looks back
and finds his lover still there;

in the way I want to believe
brothers, when I look back,
have my back. Yes,
this blue scene too Is called love;

the way one brother tenderly strokes
his fingers across the back
of the other, in the same way,
when faced with Kehinde Wiley's

"Officer of the Hussars," I want to touch
the arched back and kiss the raised ass
of the brother posed as if he nor I
should have been there—unworthy

71

of this magnitude; of the caparisoned white
steed bearing our weight; of the days
it took to get our faces right. Wrong, I'm not
in the painting; it's just him. He looks back

over the shoulder that separates us
to look down on me—to
what: threaten or
love me? I have been here all along

revising your violent strokes against me
as love. I've made enough
of your beauty
out of my own shame.

Are you clean,

one mouths to the other. Strangers,
yes, yet brothers bound
by blind need for parts they have

already. As if he has seen enough,
one turns the other around
in the narrow stall. The stainless

steel partitions already stained
in what came before.
You've been here before

on this filthy toilet,
or on another, on the floor
your eyes trained

for fresh shadows
to dirty your light;
an eye filling

an ill-fitted doorjamb
becoming a mouth gaped wide enough
to say *all* or

absolution. I'm sorry—
I know you
wanted them all—every man

who walked in
to wash hands
that never got clean.

Bareback Aubade with the Dog

Thicker than its master's thigh,
I saw that dog gnawing its leash—
and didn't I know better? Knowing my fear

of dogs, I thought, "If I walk faster
and stay calm, then—"

That leash, thin as *Yes*, snapped. Of course
the dog snapped too and I
wasn't fast enough—only two legs then

instead of four. I was afraid, yes,
though I didn't run. With my eyes shut,

I braced for what comes to those afraid
of what they refuse to see. Yet
that time, the dog headed for the lake.

It passed me by and I watched
the water gulp it down—its paws and then

its legs and then its flanks and then gone
was the scruffy heart
of its head. Wasn't I sure it would not resurface

when it did? What sunlight there was
caught in its mouth a small body—its
slim head bucked twice more
against the water's vermillion ripple.

And the dog comes back

from the lake with nothing,
just the bark

it left with—an unintelligible
agony. Isn't that, me

being the two-legged kind,
assumption and projection? A bark

sounds like a bark. A call of danger is a call
of ecstasy. It sloughs

the lake off its flanks,
sniffs the spittle of its chewed leash—

dangling from a hand
which too doesn't know any better.

Control yourself, the dog is told.

The impossible leash
stings its back. *So this is restraint*

—I think as the dog
feigns satisfaction

in the dull salt
of a featherless palm. No,

you've caught me. I'm not there. I'm the animal
still fucking in a stranger's bed.

His tongue licks my mouth. I whistle,
I do not listen.

The Runts

It's my hand—so close

it could be bitten
clean off. Tonight

he is the dog—this bedded stranger

not using his words,
not responding to any name.

He lets me keep my hand—

returns it back cleaner
than it left. I haven't learned my lesson,

I give him the other one.

No, not *could be bitten*. He bites my hand
and I howl the way something

that should not howl.

We are both dogs now,
mouthing the dark until

we are not mouthing the dark.

We are sinking in the hold
of whatever is willing to hold us.

Lycanthropy

As if I can't understand
my body is more than surreptitious pact

between nerve
                    and the crime it loves,

they've cornered me. In this light
my frame is haphazard and threatening,

even though I can't speak—their leather collar still cinched
around my neck, a silver

O-ring for each pair of eyes daring me
to attack. Each man armed

with a hot muzzle, a mouth
full of scripture and *no* to aim

onto my back—now bent
over a prayer they mistake

for a growl. In this place,
there is no common tongue,

I can't understand them,
so I can't follow the order

that follows each leash,
so they beat me

until skin becomes wound
then scab then hide.

Palmer Park

Nightfall makes liars of the pines:
where limbs should be, men fall in lust

with men. A greedy thing, I lie
to get back here; to hear the echo behind me

of footfall. Behind me, a snapped twig
becomes *Come here*. Leave me

alone, I am just trouble
turning toward trouble

for comfort. The city's din,
though all around us,

comes from so far away,
a reminder, if we want to,

we can always come back
and be civilized;

be saved. I am never safe
and one day, looking down

at what is left of me,
I may dismiss it all

as recklessness—surely, by then,
I'd have learned to care.

I do not care—the park cures
me of loneliness. Look at how,

all along, I've held this sweet man
in my mouth, as if I intend to keep him safe.

The bug

lands on my pretty man's forearm. Harmless,
it isn't deadly at all; makes his muscle flutter
—the one that gets his hand to hold mine, or
ball into a fist, or handle a gun. It's a ladybug,
or an Asian lady beetle everyone mistakes
for a ladybug—eating whatever
it lands on. My pretty man is asleep—at ease, or
plotting like the bug. Or maybe the bug
is a blowfly—eating my pretty man's tan
from his pretty arm. My man swats it
without waking, as if he's dreaming of an enemy,
or me. When my pretty man isn't asleep
he's got a temper.

       No, he is not
asleep. He's wide awake and wants me to tell you
I'm wrong. Blowflies don't eat skin,
they lay eggs on skin. He knows all about
blowfly larvae. Napoleon used them
to clean war wounds, my cold pretty man
says in that pretty way,
with his cold pretty mouth. He's eaten plenty
of bugs before. On night watch,
over there. Over there, they're everywhere.

Fable of the Beast

I

What a lucky beast I am,
when he cleans up nice

and nicks his perfect face.
I get to lick that face,

when he lets me.
In the cut's opening

I get a taste of him
from the inside

out, which is all I have
ever wanted,

to be cell-close
to him. Praise the razor's

overzealous arm;
the ease

with which it finds tenderness
in this man.

II

I am beside myself
in the mirror. *Whose body*

is this, I ask the face,
though it just returns the question

in answer. My hand strokes my beard
which strokes my chest—

a brush drawing
then redrawing the mistake

of a collarbone.
I do not trust my body's art—

every mole and skin tag
are every mole

and skin tag signaling
disease or a desire

for disease
I never want. *Who*

has ever wanted you
to belong to them, I ask

and ask back.

III

Why not take his razor
to my face

to see if I can find

beauty buried
where he tells me

there is no beauty.

IV

In a game we've played before,
he slaps me

when he means to tickle me
then apologizes

and kisses me,

yet I am confused, not
by the violence,

but the apology—
it makes me

want to die.

V

He wants back the horns
he sawed off of me,

even though my body
can't bear the thing

he wants. A shame—
I have nothing

with which to score
his glorious vibrato

when he raises his voice
at me to raise

my back so that he
can remind me

of the difference between
the shape of a man's hand

when he means to caress
and the formlessness

when he means to strike.

VI

I will offer my body to him
to beat into the man he
wants, though I am no man,

not really, he's told me so,
still maybe this time
I can be the thing he wants.

No, it is not violence
if I ask for touch

as purposeful as
the softest caress. If not
tenderness, then

let me wear his
bruises
and not be ashamed to heal.

Niggas' Revenge

This time, articulate Black penises
in unlearned white mouths. Full

Black mouths filled
with orders. Black hands, after so long

in this field, skilled at the whip.
Passed between the brothers,

the white men find instead
of "nigger," their mouths full of "sorry,"

then piss. When one brother commands
the kneeling white men to pray to God,

of course, he's speaking of himself—
each chain link and O-ring

tethering him
back to himself.

Arcane Torso on Grindr

We cannot know his legendary head,
now hidden by a peach. Yet his torso,
all ink and Equinox, is backlit from inside
the phone: hard math; a circuitry of low

fires—sexy algorithm. Otherwise
the flexed bicep could not dazzle me so, nor could
his cum-gutter's v, his barely-shaved thighs,
nor his bottle rocket all set to flare.

Not on this phone, he doesn't have any face
pics to trade, nothing above the shoulders.
But his chest—bury my face in that fur!

Would not he, were it not for the cropped selfie,
arouse like a porn star. He says *your place
or mine*. I must lie about my life.

The Weather, the Weather

"At least the sun's out," I tell the man I'm borrowing for an hour.
Of the last round of storms, I ramble off words: "rough,"
"harsh," "bad." I go on about last winter—this
day, about a year ago. Then, like that, I shut my mouth

around the rough ramble of wordlessness. *But there are always storms
drawn to the Panhandle*, I think as steel drums beg from the Key West ad
again. Bare-wristed and grinning, without a care for what day or year it is,
the man spins his hourglass wife to the score of voice-over,

steel drums—begging us to leave everything for the Panhandle, for Key West.
Always shoeless, the lovers dip; laugh at that same joke I keep wishing I could
hear through the glass. We (What? Husbands of risk; of want?) have but an hour
booked. "At least it's sunny outside." I shut the shade of the narrow window.

Now some rerun's laugh track—we must be joking. Shoeless lovers,
we dip our toes into the carpet. I shut off the lamp. I shut the blinds
like a book. "A narrow window of sunlight, but at least we'll get sunlight."
I shut my mouth; let my hand reach for his bouncing knee, his gilt finger.

What sort of bird

destroys itself the way this one does
against the windows

of this parking structure's stairwell?
I'm too shaken to go anywhere

near it and its argument
for desperation. I know

if I were a different sort of man,
I'd yank off my shirt,

fling the thing out
into the night,

through the doorway
it isn't able to find—

the doorway I found
after leaving a man's condo,

a stranger for whose face
my thumb swiped the phone screen.

I couldn't stay long
enough to learn his real name,

because I lied about the way
I looked; I wasn't the man

we both needed tonight,
so here I am,

swiping my finger across
my shirt's top button—

not really wanting to
un-wing its halves;

my breasts
prominent enough

to be suckled
not like a man's.

And the bird, no question,
is beautiful when its beak

breaks against the glass.
Not the bird really,

but its blood-blind
serenade to the bird,

on the other side of the window
returning every gesture,

that is not really a bird,
just a trick

of light and glass.
I wet my lips and blow,

yet nothing comes out.

III

Fantasia for the Man in Blue

You know that painting, right? Matisse's *Icarus*? No,
not so much a body to speak of—

a darker suggestion,

an absence of a body,
an outline

surrounded in blue—that's you. What you were,

I can see fitting the description
if you were not denied a face,

arms perhaps tattooed

with a lover's name,
a mother's face, some evidence

of having a life.

And of your manhood—
where is it? Either way the blue

has its way with you—

its constellation of small destructions
all around you,

shell casings. No, not so much

the shell—just the evidence
of the shell. A bright wound

where a heart can't possibly exist.

Icarus Does the Dishes

It leaves a mark on me when I fall
in my father's kitchen.
Only a few days it's been
of lifting him up from one place,
then putting him down somewhere else,
then driving to work for the late shift
while a nurse looks after him
for five hours, three times a week—
all we can afford. There is no choice
sometimes, I have to leave him
alone. I ignore the soreness
of the bruise taking shape on my ass,
because these dishes won't clean themselves
and Father hasn't had his bath. It embarrasses us,
especially the rolling back of his foreskin,
the veins, tiny stitches on the inside
of a Minotaur's mask, so I let him wash that part
while I look away. He does not see me
this way, on the floor. I'm twenty-five
and agile, it is no accident, but
a tantrum. I throw the dishes.
All around me, shards; a constellation—
stars for which I have no names.
We are lost. What have I done,

I'm thinking now, in telling the hospital
I can do this; I can manage just fine.
In the next room, through the wall,
he asks me if I'm okay;
if I need him to do anything?
Please die, I whisper then sweep
the stars, turn back toward the sun
soaking in the gray water.

The Suit

A small improvised explosive device,
it went right through me, yet I didn't feel
a thing. When the plucked pin missed the fabric,
how could I move? I was boot-black careful.

"Stand up straight," whispered Father as quiet
as tripwire. He ground his teeth, bone-army,
as another line was sketched where my
body should have been. "Sorry, he isn't

built right," Father told the tailor. All tots
know to stand like their dads in old war shots.
The tailor drew more hemlines, pinned new seams.
In the mirror, Father ordered me to lean

up straighter. I was a map—the lesson
of some conquered country. I'm no one's son.

Geppetto's Lament

Off to mess with what I made him, the boy
forgets he is not a boy. Forgets these

strings and this paddle, shaped like a cross, are
in my hands. You can measure a man by

his hands. See this here thumb tip? It's the width
of a glass eye. Took my bestest knife to carve

that heartwood down to a nose then a switch.
A blade sharp enough to make a man out

of any old thing. And the tip of this finger?
Is gone. The face was tricky. He's got a

sissy's nose, a daughter's lips. Not the boy
I wished for. It was all my fault. All my

math and all my measurements were off.
Ain't even enough room in him for a heart.

Of a Wicked Boy

It dreams of real boys' bodies;
the ones on the carousel braying
as each kicks the other off

his chosen horse. They're animals
threatening to buck their restraints,

trample the whimpering
organ. Of course it wants
to touch them. Why not

their skin, the splendid
bruises, the wounds, the sweet

wounds? Instead it mouths the wrong
words to their limericks as it falls
asleep beneath a tent of colluding shadows.

It dreams of their bodies taking off
by hoof in a romp. To one it begs to be

taught the game, the boy snorts, spits
in the puppets upturned face. When it comes
to, the doll finds its wet lips

warped into a grin. At its feet,
the boy who can't stop laughing

tucks the rest of himself back
inside his pants. They're *all* laughing now.
All *touching* it—a soft hand

for every stiff limb. Their big teeth
gnash at its fingers; their knives dive

over, over. Stripped of its vest and trousers,
they go for the torso, planed crotch
in search of the city of blood and nerves

only real boys have. Pinocchio holds
still, prays to their blades, "Please strike bone."

Aaron McKinney Cleans His Magnum

With the small machine, he's tender—a brush
gently worked through seven small cylinders.
Then the chambers spin—not like a dervish,
but a rotary dial: no receiver,

no one to call for help. His finger in
the trigger. His baby, upside down, plays
dead. From the small mouth he swipes a stain.
As if he's wiping a man's tear away,

he dabs an oily salve across each frown,
each furrow. This sad calculator is
built to subtract from and divide a town.
In another town, watching the heartless

Tin Man going on about the Wizard,
I laugh at the Scarecrow. The gun holstered.

Of his daughter's hair,

he makes it look easy,
my nephew. Each
plait bargained for with nothing,
only Blue Magic and a brush
—stiff as tenderness.
Tufts gathered up,
then parted into three
braids, now five—no,
more. So many
barrettes, so many
bow knockers, I've run out
of fingers. His fingers
never run out of
hair; grow more
nimble with each tricky pass
over and under and through.
So thorough yet
so gentle. "Hurts," he asks
and the little one
answers with a deep nod
into dream. He keeps moving—
one path leads into another
where there was at first
a gathered darkness. Gone giddy,

I too am at his knee; watch
the country he's mapped out.
"Take me there," I want to say,
"make me one of its citizens,
one of its daughters."
I wish I were his daughter,
held in his lap's hull as he
builds a world for me
right in the crown of my little head.
I'd get lost in sleep
too, knowing each time I'd drift away,
there his hand would be
steering me back.

Portrait of My Father

Clothing consisted of blue corduroy
slippers, blue and white striped

boxer shorts, blue Champion
sweatpants, gray diabetic

socks, gray thermal shirt.
Black with shocks of gray,

there was a mustache
and a beard. The scalp hair

was curly and black
with shocks of gray. White

sclerae around brown irides,
the eyes. Around the right eye,

a contusion. The head was normocephalic.
Dentition was natural,

with several bottom teeth
missing. There were no masses

discernable in the neck; larynx was in the midline.
Thorax was symmetrical; unremarkable.

The external genitalia
were those of a normal adult

uncircumcised male. A 1-inch circular scar
was present on the right hip.

There was a 9-inch curvilinear
surgical scar on the left upper abdomen.

Measured at 5' 11" in length
and weighed at 139 lbs,

the body was that of a developed Black male
appearing about the recorded age

of 56 years. The body was
cool, rigor mortis long since waned.

Leda

Not *ruins*, but a *construction*
I had hoped would know
better than to collapse the next time.

It hurt, still I let him marvel
at his work—the
reckless architecture

destruction leaves behind. I fought
to hold on until we were both men again
—unremarkable. Violent song—

his body thrashed and didn't I
hold it all so close as if to learn
the lesson. Oh, I was such a sturdy

beast—my back
covered in fletching.
I left it that way; knowing

neither one of us was whom we led
the other to believe. I will leave
the door open, I told him.

I never said I knew better,
there was my tongue's need
to lick my dry lip

because such an occasion
demands a whistled song to mark it.
The feathers I felt

clinging to my lips I didn't think
to pinch away; his soft cords
on the tip of my tongue—

promises of his body's return.

Hardheaded Aubade

In the way I was told to do, the door
to strangers was shut, still he opened mine—

left me alone to my own devices.
He gave his name again when I asked. What
a bad actor—I've got my lines backward,
doubled over. On top of each other,

beside ourselves. We were a looped track. We
ran wordless night's deep redundant blue. We
pled our bodies' losing arguments. We
called each other by other names. Whom we

were could never do the trick. My shirt
in his shirt in a pile. It all felt backward—
the bedroom I no longer knew. In what
else should we have dressed decency? *What is*

your name again, one of us asked. I said mine.
Closed my hand around the knob, forced the door.

The Bug Chaser

Call me an eater of butterflies dancing
myself lonely. A fat dumb animal,

my mouth a mouth mouthing
all the pretty husks: God-folded

origami: easy bodies creased and unfolding
within reach of my mouth: a song

on the tip of
my tongue—that rind of sweet ruin

ruining me good. At this hour,
there are only delicious men, painted

in night, their lips flitting in and out
of pines, promising

what cannot be promised.
But it's so dark here

who could make them out?
They'll live to be butterflies parading

with wings painted
in a delectable poison. Any animal hungry enough

would lap their hemlock
to sleep inside the shucked bells.

The Singing Head of Orpheus

"Yup, I get it,"
is a decent response,

but would you say it that way?
I mean I do, though
I want to ask—not him—

you: when his head lands
in your lap

to go on again about
this or that—
how do you answer?

He texts me a picture
of you. I wish I were you—

you're beautiful,
of course you are—
the way your mouth dog-ears

in just the right corner
when you smile

like you don't know
we know you know
you're beautiful.

Long distance, you met
in real life and see each other

more often than I see him.
"All these women on Tinder
kept telling me how they wanted

to tear me apart in bed,"
he tells me. It's a bad connection

—all static: a river
from which I collect what
pieces you leave for me.

Do you have anything

you ask, because you have
everything and nothing
or no one, not even a man
like me, will destroy that;
because I am the germ
of what you fear
of finding in yourself;
because I am a bug
to be avoided by any means—
an inconsequential body;
because whatever music my
buggy body makes is a simple
score for the bodies that really matter;
because your life matters
more than mine, you could stomp me
and who would care; because you've
done this before; because I've done this
more times than I can count;
because our bodies are records
of where we've been; because
you can see the imperfections—
mole, scar, bruise; because
our bodies are prone
to destruction; because

when a body burns it can mean
something has gone wrong;
because something is wrong
with your memory and isn't that
a symptom of something—
you've forgotten my name,
you want to stick to user-
names, you always come back;
because I always stammer when you ask,
because you know I'll let you back in.

IV

Dear Latrice Royale

Breath can bring a house down,
especially when it is attached

to song, and that song
comes from a big bad Black

man in Fenty Beauty,
tall heels, and a spotlight—

that doesn't emanate from
a bulb on a police cruiser,

with an officer who means well
to make good on a wolf ticket;

a ticket unlike the one I bought
to watch your spangled blue gown bend

the club lights as you bent my note
and tucked it in your bra.

You stole something
that made my heart ache.

The Lady Chablis as Herself

Tommey, or however you spell your name, I
mean what I say. Like how them white boys think
Whitney or somebody's going to do The Lady. Nu-uh, I
have to be her in your little poem. Boy, I could almost

smack your face—who do you think you are? Look,
only I have the pipes to speak for The Lady. Good
drag is not just a dress and a wig. You got to put this in

The Lady's words right. Because she, above anything,
is my livelihood. Chile, I'm a kept woman as long as she lets
me keep this roof I'm under; my pans full of meat. Try
to be her and you will fail. I've got years on

you, Sugar Lump. You can't just go pull something
out of a closet. Only I can make good from all her ugly.

Rest Stop in Rawsonville, Michigan

I've not managed a clear distinction
between need and want
for myself. Is it too late to go on

about loneliness or the desperation

loneliness requires? At the threshold
of every stall door so many filthy bootprints—
their wild trajectories don't make sense:

exits negate entrances

and there is no way out of this
mess of intention. I have gone dumb
with want; the same dim beast

dancing alone, stomping from footprint

to footprint, looking for a way out
through the hidden door
of a stranger's broad back.

A son of desire,

I've come to understand that
the Minotaur too gets lonely
longing for

an intruder's footfall.

In the way the field dressers do,
I want to be touched
free of this want;

knife me into what fathers hunger.

The Hunger of Luther Vandross

Honey, what would a thinner man know of hunger,
I mean to be forever, for always in hunger.

When my stomach has had enough, when my body goes quiet,
I let my mouth take over. It's a calling, this hunger

to sing for a love I'm too ashamed to want for myself, so I
practice; the pitch has to be right to sing the hunger

of other lovers, a take on a take, a rendition no one has heard
before, with this voice I wed the lives of others. A hunger

to set the mood—I make them turn the lights off,
turn them on. A gift, this first instrument of hunger;

this tenor. I can feel it in my body, all 300 pounds of me.
You're never lonely when you're a man, who knows hunger

like I do, as big as two men holding on so tight that you would think
there is only one. There are two of me, both of us hungry

for the stage. Look at how the spotlight searches for me, it can't keep up.
They chant my name; want more of me. Who am I to let them starve?

Luther Vandross Sings Bowie

There I am, the blue on blues
of a three-piece suit. A background

singer, I'm the backdrop,
the sky that threw down

what could not be understood
back to earth—this alien

from England all dressed
down in earth tones. Troposphere

to his exosphere, a space
inside of deep space,

when you hear him, you're
hearing me too. No,

you don't know me yet—
a star too far to be comprehended

as a star; just a grain of glitter
caught in the crease of Bowie's snarl

when he sings, "Just you
and your idol singing falsetto."

Troposphere to exosphere,
a body buried within a body,

my voice thickens his voice
the way distance thickens

white noise, only not noise,
an unheard signal,

a message it took a Martian
to say in order to be heard.

That fretboard soaring up from
his shoulder is not a rocket;

not the wing that survived
the fall. There is no magic

stardust. Inside that white boy
is nothing but a big bad brother.

Luther Dreams of Aretha Franklin's Gown

I have forgotten her name.
And the name of this trim—
gold tremolo at my fingertips,
ashimmer, all sun-drunk frill.

There is a word more blue
than blue, but I can't find it
here with this ruched tongue
of almost-silk or the impossible

leather of an animal I can barely
name. Even when she's on the fringe
of one note, I want to leave her enough
room in the sleeves

for her arms to show what a piano is
for. I have forgotten
what a piano is for. How am I going to sew
her neckline—a low plunge to frame her

throat, the brown flesh that shields it,
yet not forever. It's only skin.
And a voice is only a voice
to be, eventually, destroyed

and forgotten. How about a shawl
as blue as the sky that dapper diva
Lucifer fell through when God
stole his voice; stripped him of his

body; made him legless. But lucent
the blue I stroke
that is sure to leave me
if I *should* wake.

Bling Elegy

Change your name to something
wholesome, then go platinum

blond. The world is your
egg shell. When you've outgrown that

smash it against another celestial house. Go galactic
or go home to Canada. Think of Mercury

or, better still, Pluto—how quickly
one can be downgraded from his former glory.

You are a star, boy! There are legions
wanting to descend beneath the arena stage

with you holding their hand
at the end of the night. And you lead them on

through one dark corridor after another.
You are a god, baby,

baby, baby. Oh, nothing can touch you.
You know what we want—

give us the big bang.

Fantasia for the Man in Blue

What should you have expected—
it's still dark at this hour. There is a star

in the crest of his shield
too small to shield

a thing like the heart.
You're like that Matisse painting

of Icarus, you almost say
before you realize it's all wrong—

the colors all mixed up in your head.
No, you are the disobedient one

littering the spangled blue night
with your dark tear. It's wrong

to say this, you know, but the officer
is so hot. You want to kiss him

and run your fingers through
his blond hair. Sigh—just look

at the way the moon catches his metal;
he shimmers like a handsome pistol.

Notes

This book's opening epigraph was taken from the glorious and important essay collection *White Girls* by Hilton Als.

"How Sweet this Great Land": When Marion Jones, a white housewife, opened the door to see Rubin Stacy, a homeless Black tenant farmer asking for food and water, she screamed and claimed the man tried to attack her. On July 19, 1935, in Fort Lauderdale, Florida, photographs were taken of Stacy's resultant hanging.

"My God, Lick Him Clean": This poem was commissioned by the Detroit Institute of Arts for its 2019 reading series "Art is Poetry / Poetry is Art." Peter Williams' "Portrait of Christopher D. Fisher, Fourth Reich Skinhead" is the driving force behind this poem. Inspiration must also be attributed to University of Leeds professor Manuel Barcia and his lecture "White Cannibalism in the Slave Trade: The Curious Case of the Schooner *Arrogante*"—delivered at University College London in November of 2016.

"Framing Debra Shaw": The quote is taken from the book *Gods and Kings: The Rise and Fall of Alexander McQueen and John Galliano* by Dana Thomas. In Alexander McQueen's 1997 Spring show titled *La Poupée*, Debra Shaw, the legendary Black model and McQueen muse, walked the runway donning a large metal structure, sculpted into a square, with manacles inside all four corners. The piece was created by jewelry designer, and frequent McQueen collaborator, Shaun Leane.

"The Ballad of Bobby Blake": In 2001, after appearing in about 100 gay adult films, Bobby Blake retired and became a Baptist minister. More insight on Blake's journey can be found in his memoir *My Life in Porn: The Bobby Blake Story*.

"Castro Supreme Finally Speaks": Castro Supreme, who has performed in both straight and gay adult films, is featured in the gay-for-pay porn series "It's Gonna Hurt."

"Not an Elegy for Erik Rhodes": Erik Rhodes, a performer, escort, blogger, and New York socialite, was active in gay adult films from 2004 until his death in 2012.

"Niggas' Revenge": The title and inspiration for this poem comes from the controversial 2001 Dick Wadd release starring Bobby Blake and Flex-Deon Blake—both partners at the time. "Nigga's Revenge" marked Bobby Blake's final role before retirement.

"Arcane Torso on Grindr": This poem steals from Rainer Maria Rilke's sonnet "Archaic Torso of Apollo."

"Diesel Washington Demonstrates *The Bully*": Diesel Washington, a retired gay adult performer, was known for naming the sexual positions he used in his films. *The Bully* was one such position.

"Aaron McKinney Cleans His Magnum": Aaron McKinney, along with Russell Henderson, was charged in the 1998 slaying of Matthew Shepard in Casper, Wyoming.

"Of his daughter's hair": Dedicated to my nephew—Carlos Hughes.

"Portrait of My Father": All the text, with some alterations, was lifted from James Blount's autopsy report.

"Dear Latrice Royale": Latrice Royale is a drag persona created by Timothy Wilcots.

"The Lady Chablis as Herself": The last word of each line was lifted from a 1996 *Entertainment Tonight (ET)* segment with The Lady Chablis. She starred as herself in Clint Eastwood's adaptation of John Berendt's novel *Midnight in the Garden of Good and Evil*. In the *ET* segment, while trying on wigs, she proclaims, "I think I almost look good in anything. Let's try on something ugly." The Lady Chablis died in 2016.

"Luther Dreams of Aretha Franklin's Gown": Before his 2003 stroke that left him in a coma, singer Luther Vandross designed gowns for Aretha Franklin's farewell tour. Vandross died in 2005. For more on Vandross' life, see *Luther: The Life and Longing of Luther Vandross* by Craig Seymour.

"Luther Vandross Sings Bowie": This poem was inspired by David Bowie's performance of "Young Americans" on The Dick Cavett Show—aired in 1974.

Acknowledgments

First, I am grateful to the editors and staff of the following journals in which work has appeared, often in various forms: *Cherry Tree, Connotation Press: An Online Artifact, Ecotone, Four Way Review, Indiana Review, Kenyon Review, Magma, Ninth Letter, Nomadic Ground Poetry, Phantom, Poetry, The Poetry Review, Third Coast*, and *Transition Magazine*.

Ross White, Matthew Olzmann, and my Bull City Press family—thank you. It is because of your guidance, friendship, and encouragement that *What Are We Not For* (Bull City Press, 2016) exists. Without the groundwork set in that chapbook, there would be no *Fantasia*.

From *What Are We Not For*, the following poems reappear in this manuscript: "Bareback Aubade with the Dog," "And the Dog Comes Back," "The Runts," "Lycanthropy," "The Bug" as the "The bug," "The Weather, the Weather," "The Suit," "Geppetto's Lament," "Of a Wicked Boy," "Aaron McKinney Cleans His Magnum," and "The Bug Chaser."

Martha Rhodes, my teacher, my editor, and my friend: from the beginning, you saw this book before I could see it for myself. Thank you, thank you, thank you.

Thank you, Peter Williams, for blessing this book with "Portrait of Christopher D. Fisher, Fourth Reich Skinhead, 1995." I am in awe of you. Thank you.

Sharon Harrell and the Detroit Institute of Arts, thank you for inviting my work into the gallery.

Kresge Arts in Detroit, thank you for your very generous support.

I'd like to also thank the following people for their support—either directly or indirectly: A. Van Jordan, Adam Giannelli, all of you at Warren Wilson College MFA Program for Writers, Aricka Foreman, Bread Loaf Writers' Conference, C. Dale Young, Carl Phillips, Cave Canem, Cornelius Eady (without *Brutal Imagination* this book would not have happened), David Blair's undying spirit, Eduardo C. Corral, Ellen Bryant Voigt, Francine Conley, francine j. harris, Friends of Writers, Gabrielle Calvocoressi, Jamaal May, Kahn Davison, Nandi Comer, Nathan McClain, Phillip B. Williams, Scheherazade Washington Parrish, Tarfia Faizullah (for Saturdays or Sundays), The Grind, Toi Derricotte, and Vievee Francis (my first teacher and my sister).

And as always, my everlasting love to my family, especially LaShawn Hughes, LaRon Ward, and Glory and James Blount.

A Cave Canem alumnus, Tommye Blount is the author of *What Are We Not For* (Bull City Press, 2016). A graduate from Warren Wilson College's MFA Program for Writers, he has been the recipient of scholarships and fellowships from Kresge Arts in Detroit and Bread Loaf Writers' Conference. Born and raised in Detroit, Blount now lives in the nearby suburb of Novi, Michigan.

Publication of this book was made possible by grants and donations. We are also grateful to those individuals who participated in our 2019 Build a Book Program. They are:

Anonymous (14), Sally Ball, Vincent Bell, Jan Bender-Zanoni, Laurel Blossom, Adam Bohannon, Lee Briccetti, Jane Martha Brox, Anthony Cappo, Carla & Steven Carlson, Andrea Cohen, Janet S. Crossen, Marjorie Deninger, Patrick Donnelly, Charles Douthat, Morgan Driscoll, Lynn Emanuel, Blas Falconer, Monica Ferrell, Joan Fishbein, Jennifer Franklin, Sarah Freligh, Helen Fremont & Donna Thagard, Ryan George, Panio Gianopoulos, Lauri Grossman, Julia Guez, Naomi Guttman & Jonathan Mead, Steven Haas, Bill & Cam Hardy, Lori Hauser, Bill Holgate, Deming Holleran, Piotr Holysz, Nathaniel Hutner, Elizabeth Jackson, Rebecca Kaiser Gibson, Dorothy Tapper Goldman, Voki Kalfayan, David Lee, Howard Levy, Owen Lewis, Jennifer Litt, Sara London & Dean Albarelli, David Long, Ralph & Mary Ann Lowen, Jacquelyn Malone, Fred Marchant, Donna Masini, Louise Mathias, Catherine McArthur, Nathan McClain, Richard McCormick, Kamilah Aisha Moon, James Moore, Beth Morris, John Murillo & Nicole Sealey, Kimberly Nunes, Rebecca Okrent, Jill Pearlman, Marcia & Chris Pelletiere, Maya Pindyck, Megan Pinto, Barbara Preminger, Kevin Prufer, Martha Rhodes, Paula Rhodes, Silvia Rosales, Linda Safyan, Peter & Jill Schireson, Jason Schneiderman, Roni & Richard Schotter, Jane Scovell, Andrew Seligsohn & Martina Anderson, Soraya Shalforoosh, Julie A. Sheehan, James Snyder & Krista Fragos, Alice St. Claire-Long, Megan Staffel, Marjorie & Lew Tesser, Boris Thomas, Pauline Uchmanowicz, Connie Voisine, Martha Webster & Robert Fuentes, Calvin Wei, Bill Wenthe, Allison Benis White, Michelle Whittaker, Rachel Wolff, and Anton Yakovlev.